CARBON CAPTURE
and Other Climate Tech

Co-published by agreement between Shi Tu Hui and World Book, Inc.

Shi Tu Hui
Room 1807, Block 1,
#3 West Dawang Road
Chaoyang District, Beijing 100025
P.R. China

World Book, Inc.
180 North LaSalle Street
Suite 900
Chicago, Illinois 60601
USA

Copyright © 2024. All rights reserved. This volume may not be reproduced in whole or in part in any form without prior written permission from the publishers.

WORLD BOOK and the GLOBE DEVICE are registered trademarks or trademarks of World Book, Inc.

Library of Congress Cataloging-in-Publication Data for this volume has been applied for.

Cool Tech (set, hardcover)
ISBN: 978-0-7166-5479-7

Carbon Capture and Other Climate Tech
ISBN: 978-0-7166-5481-0 (hardcover)
ISBN: 978-0-7166-5493-3 (softcover)
ISBN: 978-0-7166-5487-2 (e-book)

Written by Richard Spilsbury

STAFF

VP, Editorial: Tom Evans
Manager, New Product: Nicholas Kilzer
Curriculum Designer: Caroline Davidson
Proofreader: Nathalie Strassheim
Coordinator, Design Development & Production: Brenda Tropinski
Digital Asset Specialist: Rosalia Bledsoe

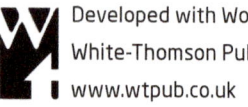

Developed with World Book by
White-Thomson Publishing LTD
www.wtpub.co.uk

ACKNOWLEDGMENTS

Cover	© Rudmer Zwerver, Shutterstock
5	© Climeworks
6-7	© Rudmer Zwerver, Shutterstock; © Sven Kaestner, AP Photo
8-9	© NTB/Alamy Images; Andrea Starr, Pacific Northwest National Lab; Jim Young, UIC Engineering; © Verdox
10-11	© Carbon Engineering; © Ashley Landis, AP Photo; © CarbonCapture
12-13	© REUTERS/Alamy Images; European Union; © Climeworks
14-15	© Carbon Engineering; © Karolis Kavolelis, Shutterstock; © Synhelion; © Michael Potts, Alamy Images
16-17	© Peter Devlin, Alamy Images; © The Earthshot Prize; © Orjan Ellingvag, Alamy Images; © REUTERS/Alamy Images
18-19	© Audi AG; © Paul J Fearn, Alamy Images; © Made of Air; © Jenson/Shutterstock; © Aether
20-21	© sakkmesterke/Shutterstock; © Science History Images/Alamy Images
22-23	© Edwin Remsberg, Alamy Images; © BP Europa SE; © Iain Masterton, Alamy Images; © Sabic
24-25	© Swift Solar; © Lio Voo, Wirestock Creators/Adobe Stock; © Vortex Bladeless; © SeaTwirl
26-27	© Gensler; © Kateryna Kon/Shutterstock; © cbpix/Shutterstock
28-29	© Xinhua/Alamy Images; © Hydrostor
30-31	© BASF; © Powin Energy; © Skeleton Technologies; © Enzinc; © Invinity Energy Systems
32-33	© Antora Energy; © Abengoa; © Quidnet Energy; Patrik Ohman, Vattenfall
34-35	© OceanTherm; © Mike Hill, Alamy Images
36-37	Brendan Kelaher, Southern Cross University; David H. Harlow, USGS; © Dezzor/Dreamstime; © Imaginechina Limited/Alamy Images
38-39	© visdia/Shutterstock; NASA; A. Treuer/ESA
40-41	© Vesta; © Scenics & Science/Alamy Images; © Hemis/Alamy Images; © Images & Stories/Alamy Images
42-43	© structuresxx/Shutterstock; © NTU Singapore
44-45	© Joep van Oppen, TU Delft; © Henri Werij, TU Delft; © Aptera Motors; © Virgin Hyperloop One; Camilo Sanchez (licensed under CC BY-SA 4.0)

CONTENTS

Acknowledgments 2

Glossary 4

Introduction 5

1. Carbon Capture 6

2. Carbon-Free Energy 20

3. Storing Power 28

4. Geoengineering 34

5. Energy Efficiency 42

Resources 46

Index 48

There is a glossary of terms on the first page. Terms defined in the glossary are in boldface type **that looks like this** on their first appearance in the book.

GLOSSARY

aerosol very fine particles suspended in the air or in some other gas. Smoke and fog are common aerosols.

albedo the amount of light reflected by a surface or material.

aquifer a layer of porous underground rock that holds water.

atmosphere the mass of gases that surrounds Earth and is held to it by the force of gravity.

basalt a hard, dark-colored volcanic rock.

carbon dioxide (CO_2) a heavy, colorless, odorless gas, present in the atmosphere or formed when any fuel containing carbon is burned.

carbon footprint the amount of carbon dioxide (CO_2) emitted due to the use of fossil fuels by a particular person, group, or activity.

electrode either of the two terminals of a battery or any other source of electricity.

fossil fuel a source of energy that formed from the remains of living things that died millions of years ago. Coal, oil, and natural gas are fossil fuels.

greenhouse gas a gas that warms the atmosphere by trapping heat of solar radiation reflected from Earth's surface, much like the glass in a greenhouse.

modular constructed in similar sizes or with similar units for flexibility and variety in use.

nanomaterial material produced using particles between 1 and 100 nanometers in size. A nanometer is one-billionth of a meter, about 3 to 5 times the size of a single atom.

photovoltaic any device or material that absorbs energy from sunlight and converts it into electricity.

renewable energy from natural resources that can be used over and over. It includes energy from the sun, from wind, from moving water, from heat beneath the ground, and from plants.

saturated a solution is saturated when no more of a substance will dissolve in it at the same temperature and pressure.

solvent a substance that dissolves another substance to form a solution.

synthetic anything made from chemical reactions that is not naturally occurring.

turbine a machine for producing power, in which a wheel or rotor is made to revolve by a fast-moving flow of air, gas, or water.

yeast a group of simple organisms known as fungi, which exist almost everywhere in nature, including the air.

INTRODUCTION

Imagine a world without global warming, where the polar ice caps aren't shrinking and coastlines are not under threat from rising sea levels. Imagine abundant power without the need for carbon-based fossil fuels. Since the industrial revolution, the world has been powered by carbon. What if a thriving post-carbon economy can emerge? All of this is possible. Remarkably, there are now ways to remove carbon dioxide (CO_2) and other greenhouse gases from the atmosphere and industrial emissions. This is carbon capture.

Carbon can be locked safely away in underground caves, layers of rock, and concrete. The captured carbon can even be used as a resource. Biofuels, novel building materials, and water purifiers are just a few products that can be made from captured carbon. Scientists are developing innovative ways to generate power, too: power that can be stored in next-generation batteries and as heat in glowing blocks of carbon! Scientists are even imagining ways to combat global warming by engineering the climate. This book looks at the ways that carbon capture and other tech are shaping the world today and how it might affect it in the future.

Could carbon capture plants of the future look like this?

1 CARBON CAPTURE

CLEANING THE ATMOSPHERE

Climate change is the most urgent problem facing our planet. **Greenhouse gases** produced by human activities are already causing global warming. And more are being emitted every second from the world's power plants, factories, automobiles, trucks, airplanes, and trains. Countries, industries, and individuals are making changes to reduce **carbon dioxide (CO_2)** and other greenhouse gas emissions. Yet urgent goals for reductions are not being met. There is no quick fix to climate change. But carbon capture combined with reduced emissions is the closest thing we have to one.

Many high-tech carbon capture solutions are now being designed and put into practice around the world. How do we capture CO_2 more efficiently? Today, most power plants capture CO_2 postcombustion. In postcombustion capture, gases from combusting (burning) **fossil fuels** go out of the flue (exhaust chimney) and pass through liquids that strip out the CO_2. This removes up to 90 percent of the CO_2 produced by burning fossil fuels.

Oxy-fuel combustion is a technology that promises to simplify postcombustion CO_2 capture in power plants. Oxy-fuel combustion burns fossil fuel cleanly with pure oxygen instead of air. Air is mostly nitrogen gas, which does not burn. Combustion using pure oxygen to burn fuel produces less waste gas overall. And this waste gas contains just CO_2 and water after the soot is removed. The pure CO_2 gas is easily collected for storage using postcombustion capture tech. That way, it is not released into the **atmosphere** as a greenhouse gas.

An engineer monitors CO_2 capture at an oxy-fuel plant.

FLUE TRAPS

Today, massive power plants use liquid chemicals to trap CO_2, so it is not released into the atmosphere. One common chemical used to trap CO_2 is called limewater (calcium hydroxide). This clear liquid turns cloudy as the CO_2 reacts with it to form chalk. This liquid or similar chemicals are sprayed from giant tanks into industrial waste gas as it goes into the flue (chimney). But scientists are developing better methods to trap CO_2 using innovative new **solvents.** The aim is to trap more CO_2 using less energy.

Advanced solvents. One standard way to trap CO_2 has been to dissolve it in a solvent called amine. Carbonate and carbamide salts are formed in the amine solution. The CO_2 can be recovered and captured from the solution when it is heated to release the CO_2 from these salts. The amide solution can then be reused. This technique uses a lot of energy—and in some plants can result in more CO_2 emissions. Advanced new solvents, such as Mitsubishi's KS-21, do not need so much heat to capture the CO_2 gas. KS-21 contains amine, but it does not evaporate or break down as quickly in cycles of use and reuse.

Low-cost CO_2 removal. The Pacific Northwest National Laboratory (PNNL) has developed a cheap way to capture CO_2. Most solvents for CO_2 capture are in solutions containing up to 70 percent water. Boiling these solutions to release the CO_2 for storage takes a lot of time and energy—especially in industrial systems that may use millions of liters of solution. The PNNL system uses CO_2 capture solutions that are just 2 percent water. These new solutions contain advanced solvents with lower boiling points. They capture CO_2 and are recycled faster using less energy. PNNL estimates that their new method can lower the cost to capture a ton of carbon from waste gas by more than 40 percent.

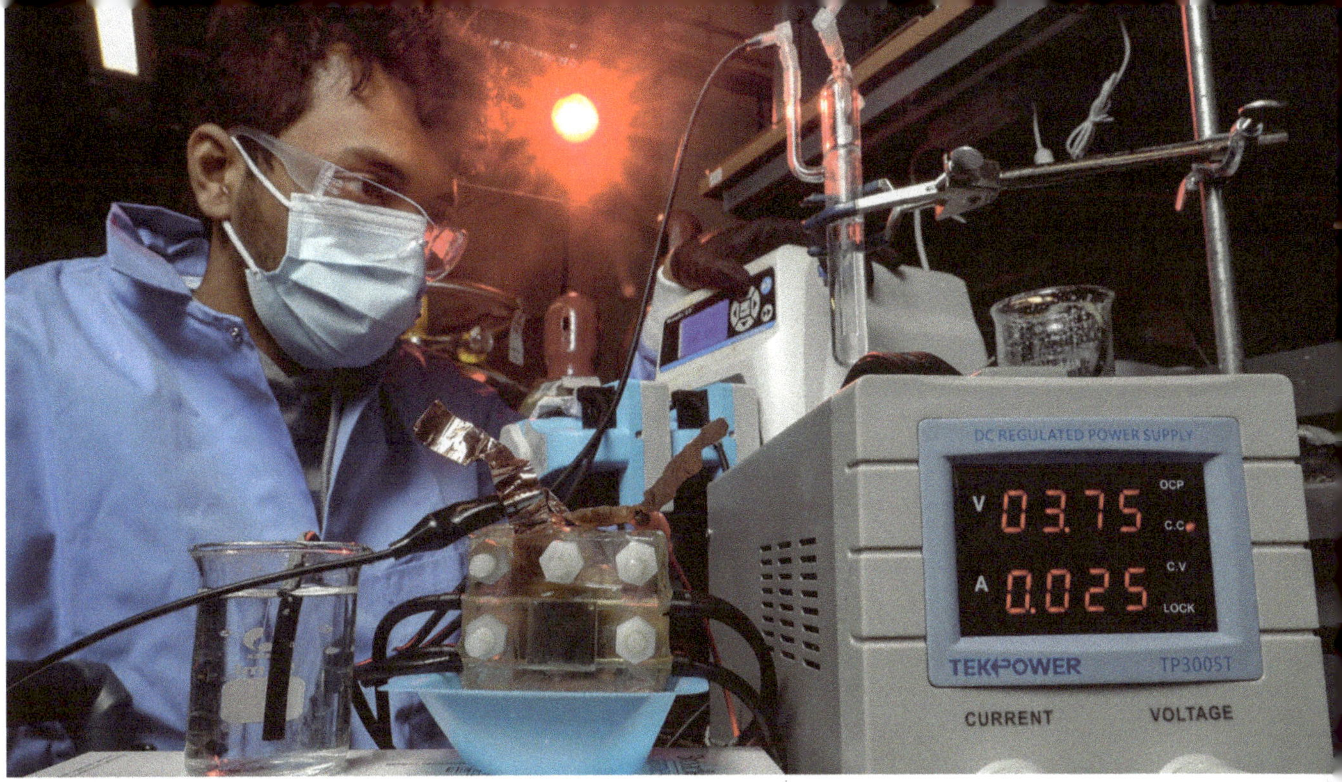

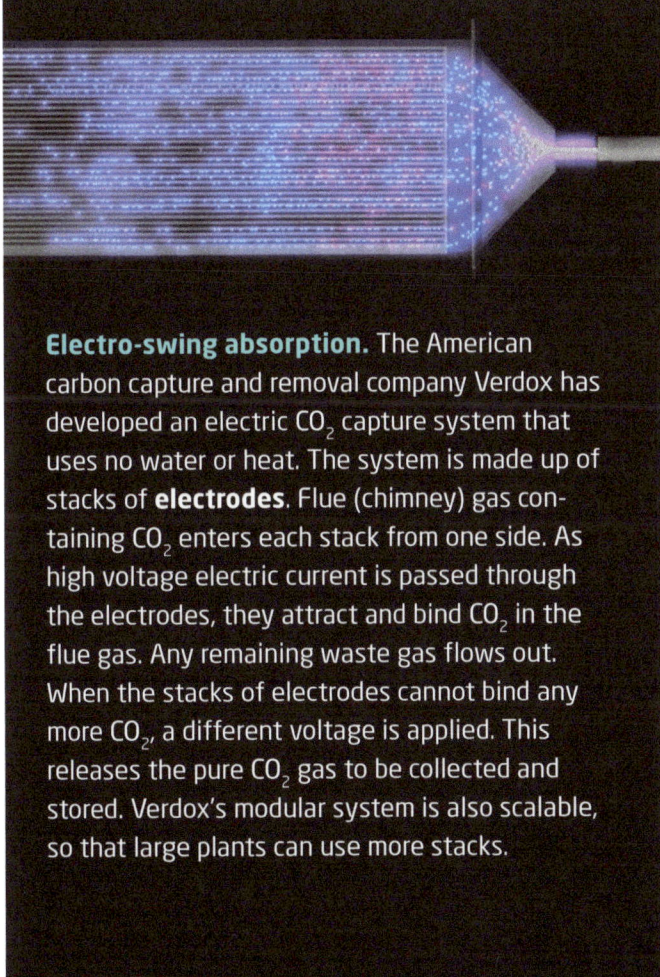

Electro-swing absorption. The American carbon capture and removal company Verdox has developed an electric CO_2 capture system that uses no water or heat. The system is made up of stacks of **electrodes**. Flue (chimney) gas containing CO_2 enters each stack from one side. As high voltage electric current is passed through the electrodes, they attract and bind CO_2 in the flue gas. Any remaining waste gas flows out. When the stacks of electrodes cannot bind any more CO_2, a different voltage is applied. This releases the pure CO_2 gas to be collected and stored. Verdox's modular system is also scalable, so that large plants can use more stacks.

Electrodialysis is a technique where CO_2 is removed from flue gas as it passes through a semipermeable membrane (layer). Scientists in Chicago have developed a carbon capture and conversion system using a membrane coated with potassium hydroxide on one side and water on the other. CO_2 in flue gas flows over the potassium hydroxide layer and forms ions (electrically charged particles) of bicarbonate. An electric field pulls the ions through the membrane to the wet side. The bicarbonate reacts with the water, releasing the CO_2 for capture. The system uses a **modular** stackable design that is easily scaled up and down to fit any size power plant or factory. This innovative technology actually produces net-negative emissions! That means that it removes more CO_2 from the environment than it generates from the energy it uses.

DIRECT AIR CAPTURE

Direct air capture (DAC) is a relatively new technology to reduce greenhouse gases by extracting CO_2 directly from the air around us, instead of removing CO_2 from industrial waste gases. In 2022, there were fewer than 20 DAC plants operational worldwide. The largest could capture around 4,000 tons of CO_2 a year. That's equal to the CO_2 produced by about 800 automobiles over one year. At that scale, DAC will never be able to remove enough CO_2 to help combat climate change. However, there are exciting new developments with DAC.

Easy scale-up. The Canadian company Carbon Engineering is developing technology to make DAC cheaper and easier by producing modular plants. They are made up of several identical units, each the size of a shipping container. The DAC systems make use of components made from existing technology, which keeps costs low. In their DAC design, air contactors (used in cooling towers at power plants) suck air into the DAC module. Potassium hydroxide flowing over thin plastic surfaces inside binds with CO_2 from the air. A pellet reactor separates CO_2-containing salts from the liquid to form pellets of pure calcium carbonate. Finally, a calciner releases the CO_2 from the pellets for storage. Pellets can be recycled to make more potassium hydroxide. Carbon Engineering's modular DAC technology can easily be scaled up to megaton capacities. This means that one DAC plant is capable of removing one million tons of CO_2 from the air per year.

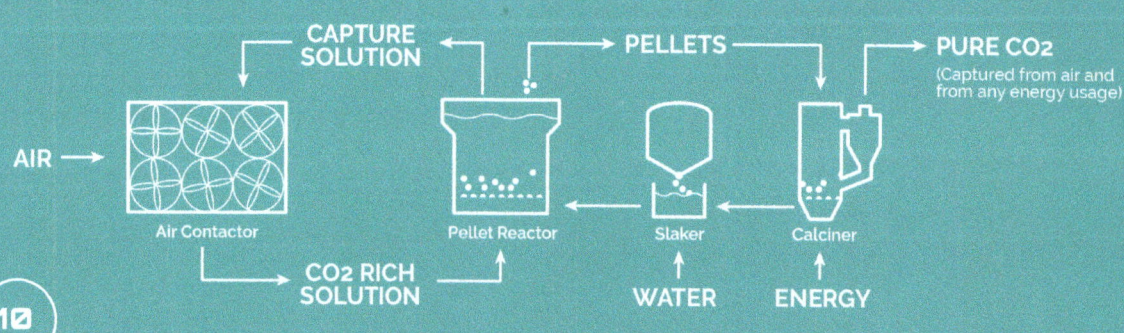

Modular reactors. Project Bison in Wyoming, USA, is a modular DAC plant that works using a different technology. Air enters through side grilles and passes through cartridges that contain multilayered air filters coated with CO_2-trapping chemicals. When the units are **saturated** with CO_2, they are heated. This releases the CO_2 for storage or use. The DAC modules can be stacked up into larger units equipped with large rotating fans to expel air after the CO_2 is removed. Modular construction means that engineers can build DAC plants of any size.

Offset with DAC. Carbon offsetting occurs when companies pay another for CO_2 removal to make up for their emissions. For example, today you can pay a little extra for an airline ticket. The extra fee is spent to plant a CO_2-absorbing tree to offset the CO_2 emissions produced by your flight. Today, some companies are offsetting CO_2 emissions with DAC credits. For example, United Airlines and Microsoft have invested in DAC plants and DAC technology. Such investments help offset the CO_2 emissions that the companies produce. The offsets are part of their commitments to becoming carbon-neutral— that is, they balance their CO_2 emissions with equivalent DAC offsets.

GEOLOGIC STORAGE

Captured CO_2 that is not used in other ways needs to be stored safely. Geologic storage uses the spaces in rock formations underground. Here, the CO_2 can be stored for long periods, and it is not released back into the atmosphere, which contributes to climate change. Today, many carbon capture plants are positioned at sites suitable for geologic storage. These are called carbon capture and storage (CCS) plants.

Underground injection. Shell Canada's Quest plant near Edmonton, Alberta, uses CCS technology for large-scale CO_2 capture from its tar sand fossil fuel reserves in Canada. Here, CO_2 from oil wells is captured and compressed into a liquid and injected (pumped) 1.2 miles (2 kilometers) into rock layers where oil was extracted. This rock is filled with tiny pores that get hold of the CO_2. Engineers monitor the watertight rock above to make sure the CO_2 does not bubble up. Many other energy companies also are injecting CO_2 underground in their depleted oil fields.

Deep saline aquifers are deep porous rock layers containing saline (salty) water. These **aquifers** are widespread, making it easier to pipe CO_2 in from nearby power plants. The CO_2 injected into the aquifer replaces salt water in gaps in the rock. In the United Kingdom, the Northern Endurance partnership is developing CCS using the massive Endurance aquifer under the North Sea. Pipes will carry CO_2 from the heavily industrialized coastal region and inject the CO_2 into a deep aquifer from an offshore facility.

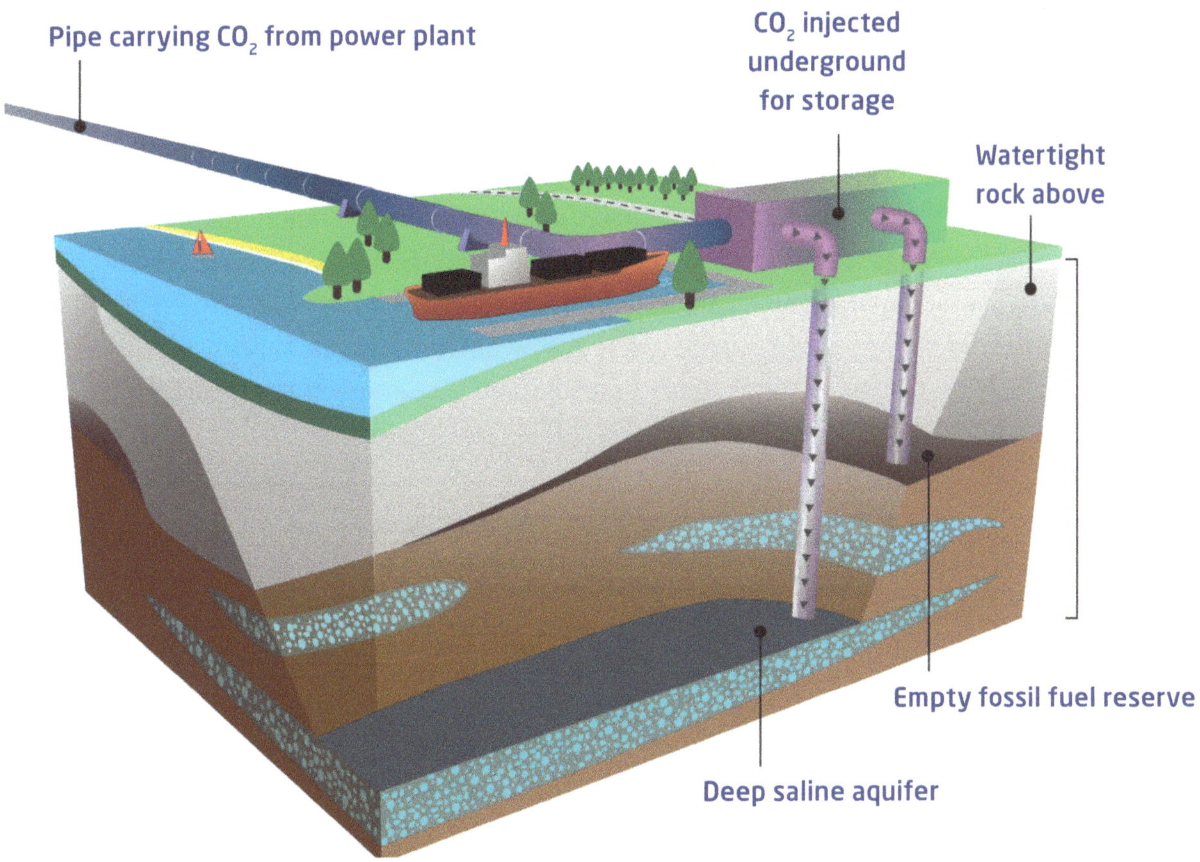

Pipe carrying CO_2 from power plant

CO_2 injected underground for storage

Watertight rock above

Empty fossil fuel reserve

Deep saline aquifer

Rock storage. The Icelandic company Carbfix specializes in storing CO_2 in layers of **basalt** deep under the ocean. This volcanic rock has lots of cracks and pores. Carbfix dissolves captured CO_2 in seawater and pumps it into basalt under the ocean. After about two years, the basalt minerals react with CO_2 to form stable carbonate minerals in the gaps. The greenhouse gas is now locked up for millions of years! The potential for CO_2 storage is enormous with basalt. Iceland is a volcanic island. New basalt is constantly formed there where molten rock emerges. Basalt is one of the most common kinds of rock on Earth's surface. It also makes up most of the ocean floor.

CCS controversy. Many governments and energy companies believe that CCS is the answer in the struggle to combat climate change. For example, Carbfix estimates that basalt could store as much CO_2 as would be produced by burning all remaining fossil fuel on Earth. But to store all that CO_2 in rocks deep underwater would cost a fortune. Today, many scientists are concerned that the technological and energy costs are too high. The funds used to develop CCS could be better spent on preserving and planting forests to store CO_2, and on energy conservation to reduce CO_2 emissions. But CCS remains an important part of global carbon reduction plans, at least in the short run.

SYNTHETIC FUELS

The vast majority of vehicles and industries today are still powered by carbon-emitting fossil fuels. New kinds of fuels are usually greener—that is, they are environmentally friendly because they release less CO_2 and other polluting gases. But what if you could make fuel to power vehicles and industry directly from captured CO_2? Such fuels would be carbon-neutral. That is, they do not increase the overall amount of greenhouse gases in the atmosphere. Exciting new technologies using captured CO_2 are emerging to create clean **synthetic** fuels that will power the future!

Aviation innovation. Norsk e-Fuel (Norway) and Carbon Engineering (Canada) have both developed processes to make aviation fuels using CO_2 captured in a DAC system. The process converts CO_2 and steam into syngas (synthetic gas) made up of hydrogen and carbon monoxide (CO). Norsk e-Fuel then streams the syngas into a reactor under high temperature and pressure. Inside the reactor, chemicals convert the syngas into synthetic e-Crude oil—very much like a fossil fuel but with fewer impurities. The e-Crude is refined into aircraft fuels used in commercial air travel. Since the e-Crude is produced from captured CO_2, the overall emissions of greenhouse gas are reduced.

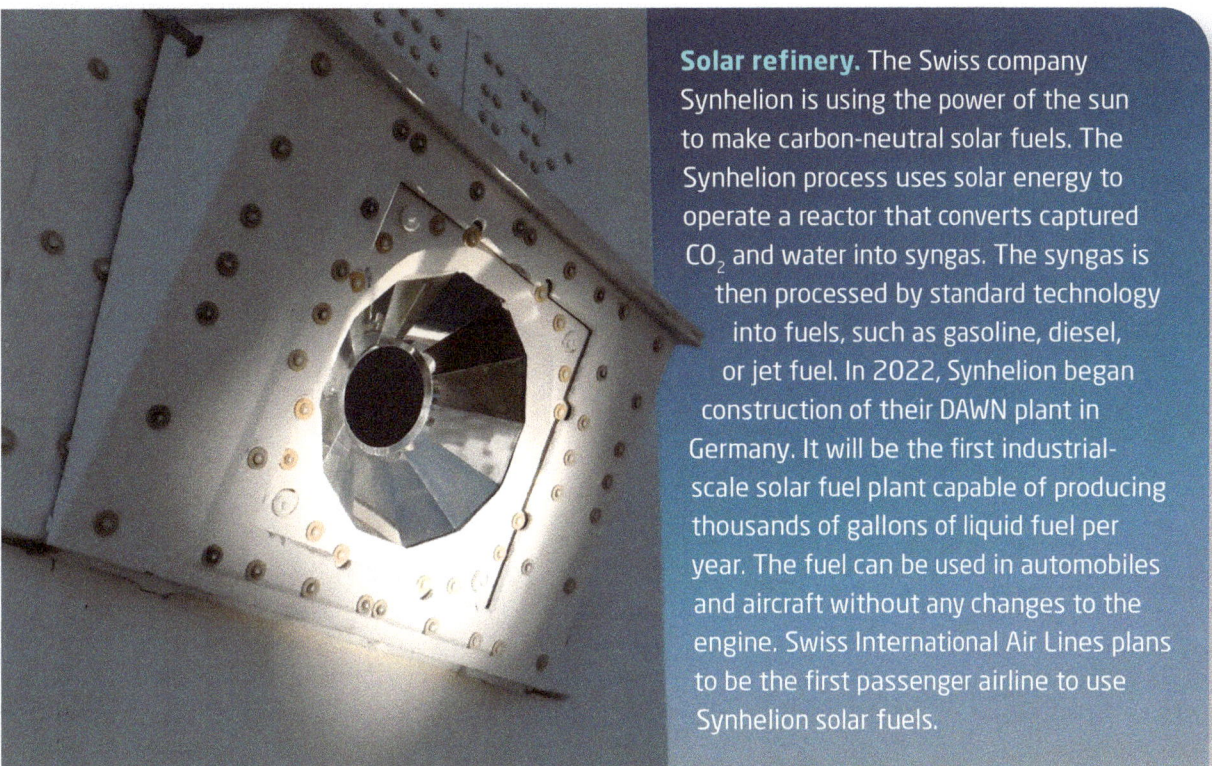

Solar refinery. The Swiss company Synhelion is using the power of the sun to make carbon-neutral solar fuels. The Synhelion process uses solar energy to operate a reactor that converts captured CO_2 and water into syngas. The syngas is then processed by standard technology into fuels, such as gasoline, diesel, or jet fuel. In 2022, Synhelion began construction of their DAWN plant in Germany. It will be the first industrial-scale solar fuel plant capable of producing thousands of gallons of liquid fuel per year. The fuel can be used in automobiles and aircraft without any changes to the engine. Swiss International Air Lines plans to be the first passenger airline to use Synhelion solar fuels.

Carbon recycling is at the heart of LanzaTech's technology. They take waste CO_2 from industrial emissions and agricultural waste and recycle it into fuels and chemicals. Their CarbonSmart technology uses bacteria to ferment the gases to make ethanol, a kind of alcohol. The process works a bit like the way **yeast** converts sugar into ethanol to make beer. **Renewable** ethanol can be blended with fossil fuels for use in vehicles, reducing the net emissions of greenhouse gases produced by burning the fuel.

F1's green revolution. Formula 1 (F1) race cars will be powered completely with synthetic fuels by 2026. German F1 manufacturer Porsche is working with Siemens and ExxonMobil to build a synthetic fuel plant in Punta Arenas, Chile. Captured carbon and hydrogen produced using wind power are used to make a kind of alcohol known as methanol, which is modified to make fuel that emits 90 percent less CO_2 compared to gasoline. The synthetic fuel developed for F1 can also be used in standard automobiles. The F1 racing industry is using its high profile to help popularize renewable synthetic fuels for everyone.

USING CAPTURED CO_2

Reducing CO_2 emissions from industry and other sources is essential to combat climate change. Carbon capture technology is also important to achieve that goal. But what do we do with all that captured carbon? Today, there is already an enormous volume of captured CO_2 available for use. Industries are already using CO_2 in innovative new ways to produce a variety of products.

Better cement. Imagine the world around you without concrete. Cement is the vital bonding ingredient in concrete. The American company Fortera has developed its Re-Carb process using captured CO_2 to make stronger cement. Cement is normally made by heating calcium carbonate (limestone) into a material called lime. This process releases CO_2. So much cement is made globally that cement production alone releases 7 percent of all CO_2 emissions in the world! Fortera wants to reduce that number. They heat natural limestone and dissolve it in a special solvent. Captured CO_2 from this process is bubbled back into the solvent to make reactive calcium carbonate used to make cement. Their Re-Carb process creates interlocking, needle-shaped connections between the cement particles, making it extremely strong and hard. These same connections are what make coral reefs so hard!

Carbon into soil. The Indian company Takachar has developed a small-scale, practical device to reduce CO_2 emissions from farming. Plant and animal waste (biomass) from farms releases great amounts of CO_2 and other greenhouse gases as it decomposes. Takachar has developed technology that burns this waste under controlled conditions to start a process called pyrolysis, where the material burns at high temperatures with little oxygen. About 10 percent of the energy generated from burning biomass is used to keep the reaction going. The controlled burning converts the biomass into a CO_2-trapping substance called *biochar*. Biochar is a valuable soil conditioner for farmers and is used in the production of rubber and paint. Farmers can use a Takachar device to make biochar at their farm using anything from scrap wood to animal dung. This saves on the cost of transporting waste to a central biochar plant. Farmers can create useful biochar instead of burning their waste. This helps reduce air pollution as well as CO_2 emissions.

Enhanced oil recovery (EOR) includes pumping CO_2 into oil wells to get more oil out of them. Oil is a sticky, heavy substance. Some oil remains in underground spaces after drilling. In EOR, CO_2 dissolved in water is pumped under pressure into oil-bearing rock. The high-pressure solution flushes out trapped oil that is recovered at the surface. EOR technology can produce 20 percent more oil from a well than just drilling alone. Oxy is an offshoot of Occidental Petroleum Corporation. Oxy uses DAC technology to generate CO_2 used for EOR at oil wells. The oil produced from such operations is sold as "net-zero oil." This means they inject the same volume of captured CO_2 that is emitted for each barrel of oil produced. However, critics point out that such technology simply prolongs our use and dependence upon the fossil fuels that drive climate change.

Growing plants. In Switzerland, captured CO_2 is being used to grow crops. Climeworks runs a DAC facility at a garbage incinerator in Zurich. Burning garbage provides the power their equipment uses to capture CO_2 created by the waste. That captured CO_2 is then pumped into glasshouses, where it is taken up by tomato and cucumber plants. Plants naturally take up and store CO_2 during photosynthesis. This way, the CO_2 is recycled in useful ways instead of being released into the atmosphere.

CARBON TO VALUE

Carbon dioxide CO_2 has usually been viewed as an industrial waste product. It was disposed of by simply floating away into the atmosphere through a chimney or smokestack. Today, more industries see captured CO_2 as a valuable raw material to be used. Some are developing innovative technology and processes to gain value from captured carbon.

Materials. Innovative tech companies are turning CO_2 into carbon **nanomaterials**. For example, Carbonova produces solid carbon nanofibers from captured CO_2 and methane, a powerful greenhouse gas. Carbon nanomaterials are 40 times stronger and many times lighter than steel. They can be combined with other materials to make materials with different properties. For example, nanofiber-reinforced plastic is tough and flexible. The Boeing Dreamliner airplane is made using this material. Using this light material rather than metal cuts the cost of fuel because it takes less energy to keep a lighter aircraft airborne. Carbon nanomaterials also conduct electricity as well as metals do.

Air materials. The Audi building in Munich, Germany, is covered with tough, waterproof carbon sheets. This building material was produced by a company named Made of Air. Made of Air produces the carbon sheets from biochar made from low-value waste wood. CO_2 is captured naturally in wood from trees. The Made of Air process locks more carbon away than it releases through power use.

Air diamonds. The Indian company Aether grows diamonds using CO_2 from DAC. The CO_2 is made into a chemical vapor and deposited as layers of diamond in a special reactor. Laboratory-grown diamonds normally use CO_2 obtained from fossil fuels. Mining natural diamonds uses a vast amount of energy to operate machinery. Aether estimates that making one small diamond removes around 20 tons of CO_2 from the atmosphere.

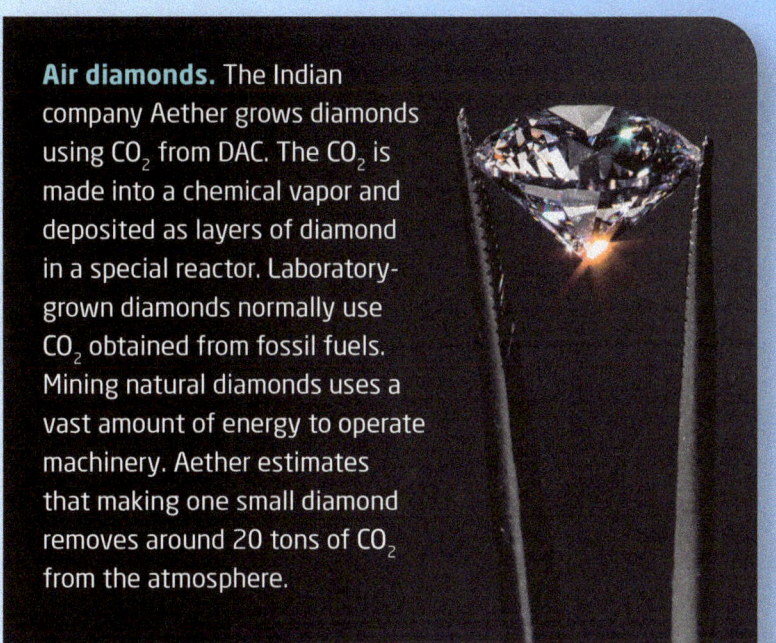

Water purification. Freshwater treatment plants use chemicals known as flocculants to remove sediments from the water. The flocculants are usually made from fossil fuels. Mars Materials is using a new process to make the flocculant acrylamide from captured carbon and corn biomass. The process was developed by scientists at the National Renewable Energy Laboratory (NREL). The process delivers higher yields of clean water. It uses less energy to produce and is less polluting than producing acrylamide from fossil fuels.

Carbon to solar panels. China is a world leader in the production of **photovoltaic** (PV) cells used to generate solar power. A new plant in Jiangsu will soon be producing a key component for solar panels using captured carbon. Sailboat Petrochemical is collaborating with Carbon Recycling International to construct a CO_2-to-methanol production facility. The facility uses CO_2 from Sailboat's industrial plant. The methanol produced can be used to make the plastic ethylene vinyl acetate, or EVA. EVA layers are used to protect the delicate PV cells. They make solar panels durable against shocks and vibrations during installation and from high winds.

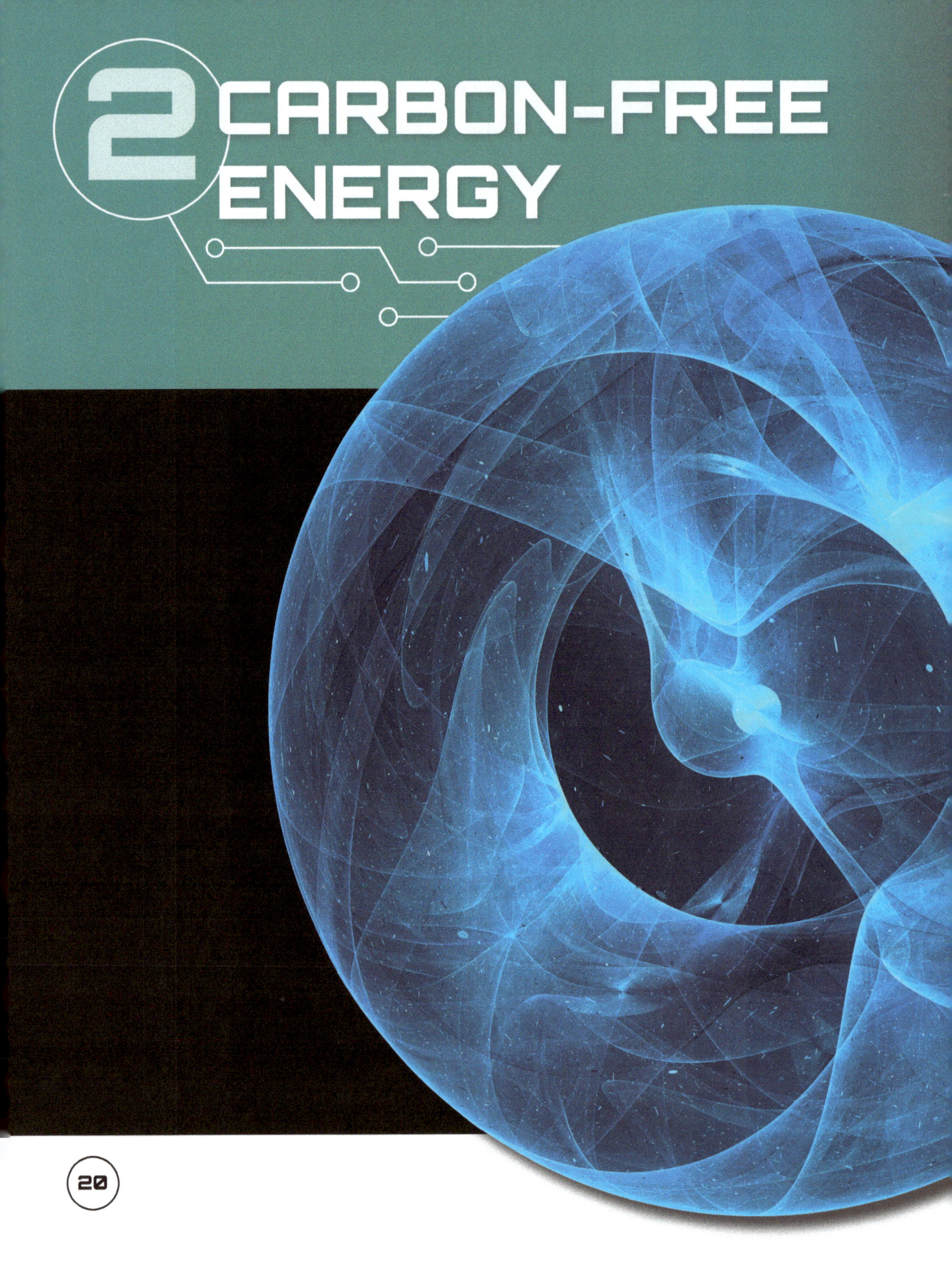

2 CARBON-FREE ENERGY

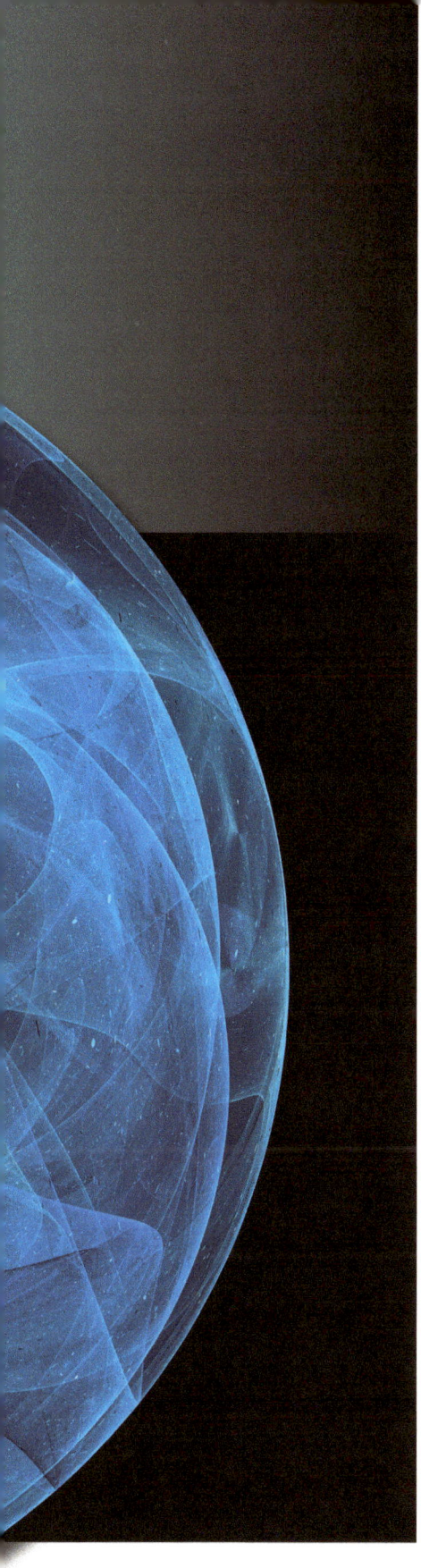

FUSION FUTURE?

The world today runs on energy. Much of that energy is produced in plants that burn fossil fuels and release enormous amounts of CO_2 into the atmosphere, driving climate change. But energy and power can be generated in many ways without carbon emissions. Carbon-free energy sources include wave, solar, wind, hydrogen, hydro, and nuclear power. No source is perfect. But new technologies are improving carbon-free or low-carbon energy production. One of the most tantalizing options for future zero-carbon energy is nuclear fusion.

Nuclear fusion occurs when heat and pressure cause hydrogen atoms to fuse (combine), releasing vast amounts of energy. The hydrogen fuel for a fusion reactor comes from seawater—an almost unlimited supply exists. One pound (0.5 kilogram) of fusion fuel releases as much energy as 10 million pounds of fossil fuel with no CO_2 emissions.

But the technological challenge of fusion power is enormous. Scientists have not yet developed a practical power plant that generates reliable power from hydrogen fusion reactions. In 2022, however, researchers at the National Ignition Facility in California reached a major milestone when they achieved *energy gain* in an experimental fusion reactor. Energy gain means the reactor produced more energy than that needed to start the fusion reaction. Fusion reactors today remain highly experimental. But nuclear fusion promises potentially limitless carbon-free energy to power our future.

HYDROGEN

Hydrogen can also replace fossil fuels in vehicle engines and power plants. Hydrogen is the most abundant substance in the universe. It burns cleanly and produces pure water as waste. But to obtain pure hydrogen, it must be separated from other substances. Today, most hydrogen fuel is made by treating methane from natural gas with steam. This process uses energy and releases about 10 tons of CO_2 for every ton of hydrogen produced—that's not exactly carbon-free! But researchers are developing new ways to produce hydrogen fuel for our carbon-free future.

Better hydrogen. A different way to produce pure hydrogen fuel is methane pyrolysis. In this process, methane is heated to high temperatures and splits into hydrogen and solid carbon. No CO_2 is released in this process. The methane used can come from natural sources—including livestock manure from farms.

Green hydrogen is hydrogen made using renewable energy sources that do not release CO_2. The BP Lingen Green Hydrogen project in Germany uses a process called electrolysis to split water atoms into hydrogen and oxygen. This is not a new or novel process, but scaling it up to the size of a power plant is a major technological challenge. BP's Lingen plant has at its heart a giant 100-megawatt electrolyzer. Lingen will use abundant power from an offshore wind farm to run its electrolyzer. Wind power is renewable and carbon-free. By 2025, the plant expects to generate about 2 tons of pure hydrogen per hour with zero CO_2 emissions.

Blue ammonia. Pure hydrogen gas is usually turned into a liquid for storage and transportation. Liquid hydrogen must be kept at low temperatures and under high pressure—and that is expensive. Aramco solves the problems of storing and transporting liquid hydrogen by using blue hydrogen. Their process extracts hydrogen from natural gas while the resulting CO_2 is captured and stored. The hydrogen is combined with nitrogen to make liquid ammonia. This liquid is easily stored and transported. The ammonia is then easily turned back into hydrogen fuel.

Hybrid hydrogen. Electric cars today are more popular than hydrogen-powered automobiles due to their plug-in simplicity. The French automaker Renault has developed a new hydrogen-electric hybrid engine that offers the best of both! Their hybrid automobile can be plugged in to charge the battery. When the battery runs down while driving, a HYVIA H2-TECH fuel cell takes over and powers the vehicle. The fuel cell combines hydrogen fuel with oxygen from the air to generate carbon-free power that emits only heat and water. The hydrogen fuel cell engine also recharges the battery while driving.

SOLAR AND WIND POWER

Solar power and wind power are well-established energy technologies that emit no CO_2. Solar or photovoltaic cells convert the energy in sunlight directly into electrical energy. **Turbine** blades convert wind energy into the movement that turns a generator. Some of the newest technology uses novel materials and designs to make these carbon-free energy sources even better.

Next-generation PV. Nearly all photovoltaic (PV) cells used to generate solar power today are made from wafers of crystalline silicon. These wafers are fragile and are usually placed under heavy glass to protect them. They are also inefficient. Modern PV cells convert only about 18 percent of the energy in sunlight into power. New PV cells made from perovskite minerals are more efficient, lighter, and more flexible. They convert about 25 to 30 percent of sunlight into usable power. Perovskite is cheap and abundant, but it often contains poisonous lead, and it can lose power over time.

Swift Solar has developed a more stable perovskite PV cell. These new solar cells use two thin layers of perovskite blended with other materials with no lead. Each layer absorbs more energy from available sunlight. The perovskite layers can be applied to almost any surface to generate electricity, from flexible garments to automobile tops!

Ultraviolet and visible light absorption

Red and near-infrared light absorption

Superheated solar thermal. Solar thermal plants generate large amounts of usable electricity from sunlight—they are a well-established technology. But today, the most efficient solar thermal plants use a novel material called supercritical CO_2 to capture the energy from sunlight. Supercritical CO_2 has the density of a liquid but moves like a gas. CO_2 can only become supercritical at very high temperatures. Most materials used to make the pipes and heat exchangers in the solar thermal plant would melt or expand under the heat. Solar thermal plants must use new tungsten and zirconium carbide materials that remain stable at high temperatures. These new materials are easy to manufacture in any shape, and they store heat well. The new materials are so efficient, supercritical CO_2 solar thermal plants can even generate power efficiently at night.

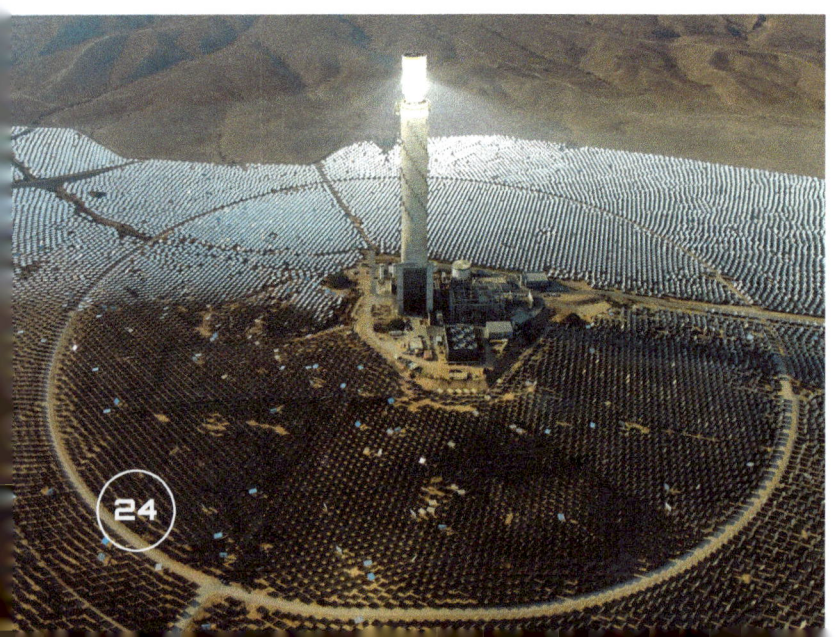

Hurricane-safe wind turbines are a necessary new technology to generate carbon-free wind power as climate change causes more extreme weather. SeaTwirl is a vertical-axis wind turbine for offshore use. Regular turbines operate in winds from one direction only. But SeaTwirl's three blades can withstand powerful winds from any direction. SeaTwirl remains stable even in rough seas while anchored firmly to the seafloor. It generates power efficiently, and the turbines can be placed close together. So a SeaTwirl wind farm occupies less area compared to traditional offshore wind power facilities.

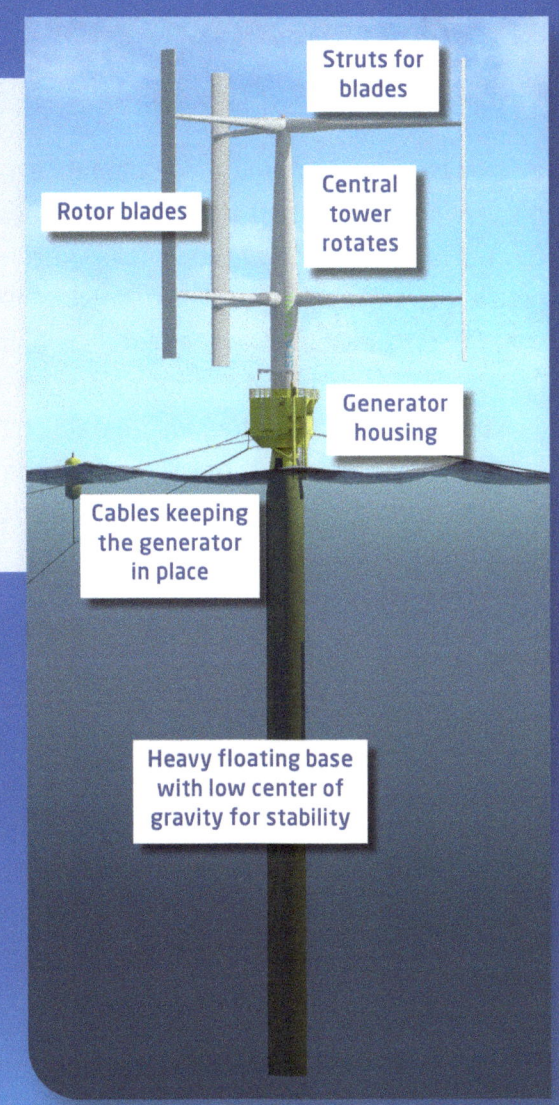

Beyond blades. Some next-generation wind power devices have no blades! Wind blowing around any structure forms spinning masses of air. These can make a wind power turbine or other structure vibrate. The Spanish company Vortex Bladeless has developed a wind power generator that uses a fixed base connected to a mast by a carbon fiber rod. The mast vibrates even in low winds. Magnets and wire coils in the mast convert the vibrations into electric power. These bladeless wind power generators can be placed anywhere—even on busy streets.

BIOFUEL AND NUCLEAR

Biofuel is an energy-producing substance made from living materials, such as plants. The materials for making biofuels can be regrown every year. So, biofuels are a renewable form of energy. Biofuel is a carbon-neutral technology—that is, it does not increase the overall amount of greenhouse gases in the atmosphere. Growing plants used for biofuels remove CO_2 from the air. But that CO_2 is released when the biofuel is burned. Carbon-neutral energy tech is just as important as carbon capture to power the future and combat climate change.

Nuclear power is another well-established energy technology. Nuclear energy is carbon-free, so it will have an important role in the future of the energy production needed to combat climate change. But nuclear power also produces dangerous radioactive waste. New technology is needed to increase biofuel production and make nuclear power safer to power our carbon-free future.

Coral inspiration. Algae are simple plantlike organisms that produce lipids (fats) that can be made into biofuels. Devices called bioreactors use light and nutrient solutions to grow algae for biofuels. But modern bioreactor designs have limitations—some algae are shaded by others in a container, reducing biofuel production. New bioreactors solve this problem with designs based on coral polyps—the tiny sea creatures that make up a coral reef. Coral polyps have a natural shape that allows the algae inside to harvest as much sunlight as possible. Scientists have designed a coral polyp-shaped frame for the algae living in a bioreactor to maximize solar energy capture and turn it into biofuel. The framework is made of crystalline material that scatters light, so each alga is exposed to even more light.

Trash power. The timber and farming industries produce a lot of trash plant material. These include branches and chippings and plant husks or stems. These tough materials are usually broken down into biofuel using heat, which wastes a lot of energy—making the process less carbon neutral. New production methods use tiny yeast cells to break down plant material into biofuel. Scientists today use genetic engineering to create varieties of yeast that can withstand exposure to the biofuel that normally kills yeast. The genetically modified yeasts can divide and grow more cells more easily in the presence of biofuel. No carbon-releasing heating is needed!

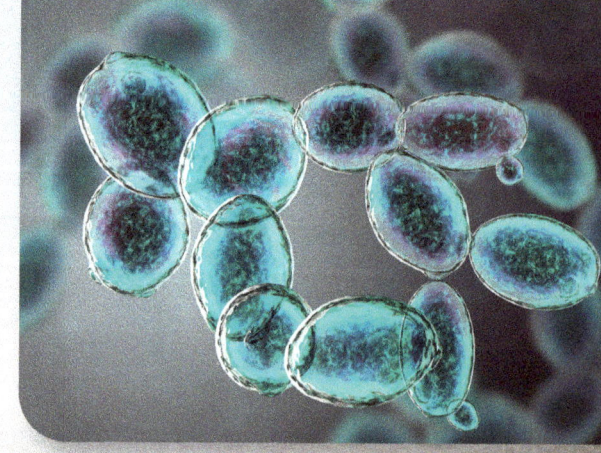

Small modular reactors, or SMRs, are the future of carbon-free nuclear power. Traditional nuclear power plants are big, complex, and costly. They produce large volumes of hazardous waste and heat. Several SMRs together can make the same amount of power. But each one is a smaller, safer, self-contained system. An SMR can be built at one location, and the complete unit can be transported and installed where it is needed—or it can be used to replace an old fossil fuel power plant. An SMR typically needs less water and complex systems to operate, and it requires little maintenance.

Neighborhood nukes. In remote locations, oil-burning generators are the only available power sources. Aurora micro-SMRs made by a California-based company named Oklo are alternatives. These small cabin-shaped reactors generate carbon-free power using waste fuel from conventional nuclear reactors. The small reactors can be placed in remote locations. Each Aurora powerhouse generates 1.5 megawatts of electricity—enough to power a neighborhood.

3 STORING POWER

POTENTIAL ENERGY

The world energy economy relies on a constant power supply to meet constant demand. Some current carbon-free energy technologies, such as wind power and solar power, do not generate power continuously— which is a major drawback. But the carbon-free energy they produce can be stored to produce power when it is needed. New technology to store energy will have an important role in the low-carbon and carbon-free energy production of the future.

One cool tech way to store energy is the flywheel energy storage system (FESS). In a FESS, excess power from wind or solar drives a motor to rotate a heavy carbon fiber flywheel. The flywheel works like a spring and converts the energy of motion into stored potential energy. When power is needed, the wound-up flywheel spins in the opposite direction. This spinning turns a generator.

Compressed air energy storage (CAES) relies on storing air under pressure. In a CAES system, air is pumped under high pressure into an underground space, such as an abandoned salt mine. When power is needed, the compressed air is heated, so that it expands into a special generator. Fossil fuels are typically burned to heat the air, so this process is not carbon-free. The Canadian company Hydrostor has developed an advanced CAES system that uses water heated by the energy released as air is compressed. This simple step can increase the efficiency of the traditional CAES process by around 25 percent—reducing the overall **carbon footprint** of the system.

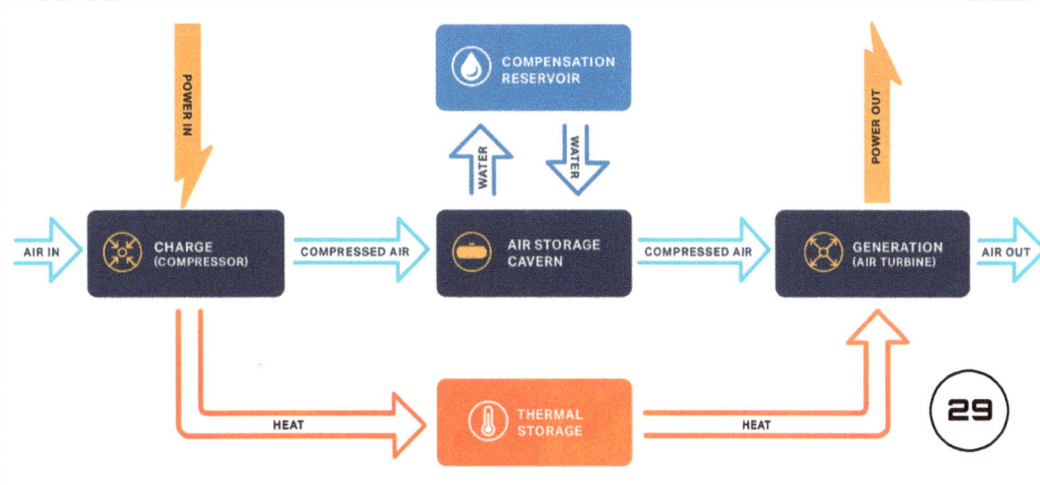

BATTERIES

Batteries will be essential in the carbon-free energy production of the future. A modern home using solar panels to generate carbon-free electricity normally stores any excess power in a large battery for use when the sun is not shining. Today, large-scale battery plants are replacing individual home batteries to store power for an entire neighborhood or town. Battery technology is also improving. New batteries are made from sustainable materials. They have better charge capacities and can be recharged more often and more quickly than ever before.

The world's most powerful battery is the Waratah Super Battery in Australia. It is an energy storage hub connected to an offshore wind farm. The battery can store and output around 700 megawatts—the amount produced by a small fossil fuel power plant. Right now, the battery does not replace any power plants. It is mainly used to generate emergency power if bushfires or lightning strikes interrupt the flow of power.

Less lithium. The most advanced batteries today use the common metal lithium to store electricity. But the global supply of lithium is shrinking. Mining lithium also creates pollution and uses a lot of water and energy. New battery technology replaces lithium with other substances that are more sustainable and better for the environment. Sodium-sulfur batteries can be made from materials extracted from seawater. These new batteries have a high energy storage capacity and long-life performance without the drawbacks of lithium batteries.

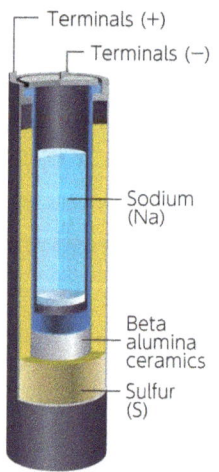

Terminals (+)
Terminals (−)
Sodium (Na)
Beta alumina ceramics
Sulfur (S)

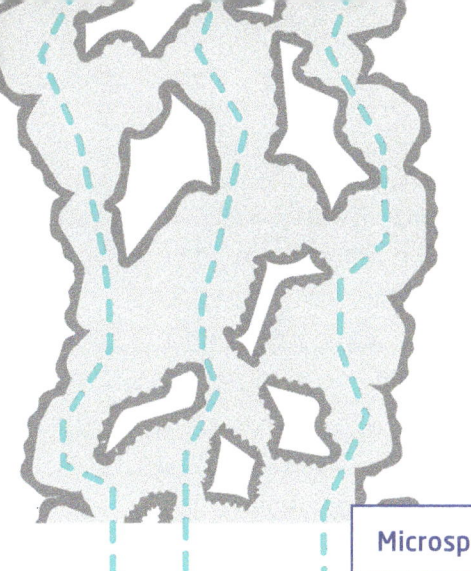

New electrodes. Rechargeable batteries are always more environmentally friendly compared to disposable batteries. Lithium batteries today replaced older nickel-zinc rechargeable batteries, which had many flaws. But they may come back as new nickel-zinc battery technology overcomes those flaws. California-based Enzinc has developed an advanced rechargeable battery that uses electrodes made from a "microsponge" of tiny zinc particles. Their new-generation zinc batteries are an inexpensive and sustainable alternative to lithium batteries. They perform as well as lithium batteries and can be recharged time after time.

Microsponge technology keeps pathways open for power to keep flowing.

Novel electrodes. Supercapacitors are devices that store energy as electric fields instead of chemical reactions as in traditional batteries. This allows them to capture and release energy incredibly fast. Estonia's Skeleton Technology SuperBatteries have ultracapacitor electrodes made of curved graphene, a novel form of pure carbon. This advanced material creates a large surface area that translates into greater energy density, or battery performance—perfect for the carbon-free energy needs of the future. Their batteries can be fully charged in 60 seconds more than 50,000 times!

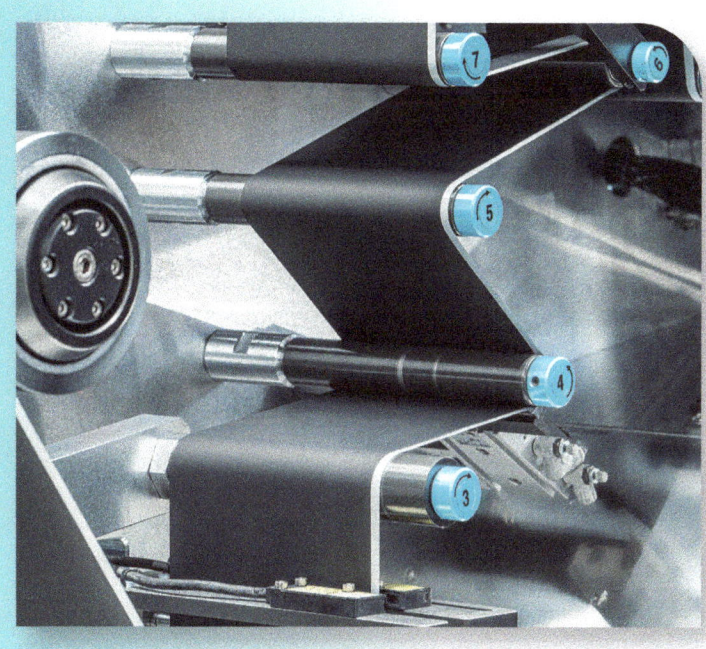

Modular battery plant. Invinity Energy Systems makes large battery modules for battery plants using vanadium flow technology. Each module contains a tank of a liquid vanadium solution that stores electrical energy. The liquid is pumped through a device that converts it into power when needed. These innovative new batteries can be used and recharged thousands of times. The new batteries are safer, too, since unlike lithium, vanadium is nonflammable.

POTENTIAL POWER

Power generated from carbon-free sources can also be stored by converting it into other nonelectric forms of energy. New technologies today can store power as thermal energy (heat). Others store water or hydrogen used to generate power. They convert the stored power into mechanical energy to drive turbines to generate electricity when it is needed.

Thermal batteries. California-based Antora Energy uses excess solar and wind power to heat blocks of carbon to over 2700 °F (1482 °C.) The blocks are then stored in insulated containers ready for use. Energy stored in the blocks can be converted into electricity using Antora's thermo PV technology. This uses special PV cells that generate power from light given off from the blocks. The thermal energy in the blocks can also heat water to make steam used to generate electricity in traditional power plants.

Salt reserve. The intense heat produced by power plants can be stored as molten salt—a clear liquid of melted sodium and potassium nitrate. Natrium energy technology uses heat from the cooling system of a power-generating nuclear reactor to make this liquid. The Hami Thermal Energy Storage System in China uses solar power to heat the salt. The liquid is pumped to a tower where sunlight reflected from more than 14,000 mirrors is focused! The heat stored in the molten salt is ready for use to generate power whenever the demand for electricity surges.

Geomechanical pumped storage (GPS) stores water under high pressure deep underground as a potential power supply. GPS systems by Quidnet Energy pump water down into deep wells that are sealed when full. When the well is opened, the high-pressure water can be used to drive turbines and generate electricity when it is needed to meet high power demand.

Hydrogen stores. Empty caverns that once held natural gas or salt can be refilled with hydrogen. Electrolysis plants on the surface make carbon-free hydrogen using renewable energy. Most of this hydrogen is used to generate power or to fuel vehicles. Any excess hydrogen is stored underground until needed—making hydrogen as available as other carbon-based energy sources. In Sweden, the HybrIT program plans to burn stored hydrogen in advanced steel-making plants. The cavern for hydrogen storage will have a special lining that prevents hydrogen from escaping. The innovative lining also prevents the stored hydrogen from reacting with natural minerals to form harmful hydrogen sulfide gas.

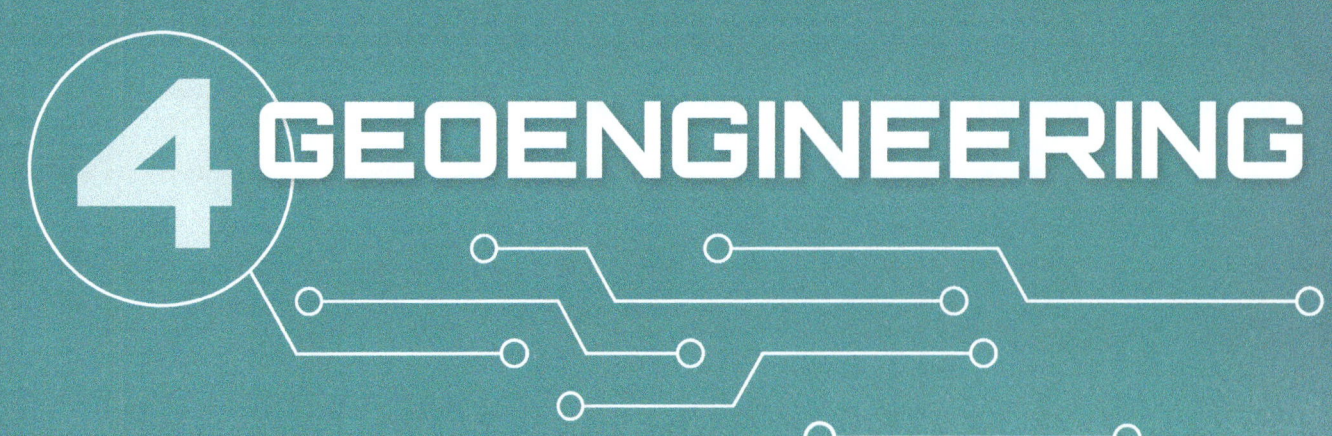

4 GEOENGINEERING

ALBEDO ADVANCES

Human technology has developed to the point where geoengineering is possible to address such global challenges as climate change. Geoengineering means interfering with natural Earth processes to manipulate the climate. This radical idea is a potential quick fix for reducing the disastrous impact of climate change. But geoengineering could upset the delicate balance of processes that regulate Earth's climates in unpredictable ways. It is a risky solution for a global problem.

But modest geoengineering is already an important part of our technological response to climate change. In hot climates, buildings are usually painted white to keep them cool by increasing **albedo.** Many scientists think that the impact of global warming can be reduced by increasing Earth's albedo to reflect more heat from sunlight into space. Some proposed methods are simple, such as planting crops that have waxy leaves that reflect sunlight. Other methods involve covering thinning Arctic ice with glass powder to reflect sunlight, lowering the temperature there. A company named OceanTherm has successfully demonstrated that using bubbles of compressed air pumped deep under the ocean pushes cold water up to cool warm surface waters. The company proposes that this technology can help prevent damaging hurricanes, which originate in warm tropical ocean waters. Cooling ocean water in select regions could reduce the frequency of these extreme weather events!

SOLAR GEOENGINEERING

One way to cool Earth is to limit the amount of sunlight that reaches our planet. Today, geoengineers are developing ways to use clouds as a natural sun screen for Earth. The idea is not as silly as it may sound. Clouds reflect sunlight into space. More clouds mean less heat energy trapped in Earth's atmosphere. Global warming would slow, stop, or even reverse. Scientists know that other chemicals in the atmosphere can act as a natural sun screen and cool Earth. For example, the 1991 eruption of Mount Pinatubo in the Philippines blasted a huge cloud of ash and gas high into the atmosphere. Earth's average temperature dropped by 1 °F (0.55 °C) over the year following the eruption.

In the atmosphere. The Mexico-based company Make Sunsets plans to combat global warming by mimicking the effects of Mt. Pinatubo! In 2023, the company tested technology using reusable balloons to spray sulfur particles high in Earth's atmosphere. The particles create an **aerosol** of sulfur dioxide (SO_2) that scatters and absorbs sunlight, so less reaches Earth, cooling the planet. Some scientists think that this technology could reverse global warming. But this would take a truly enormous number of balloons. The 1991 Mt. Pinatubo eruption blasted around 15 million tons of SO_2 into Earth's atmosphere. Researchers calculate that it would take 175,000 balloon flights in one year to lower polar temperatures by as much. SO_2 is also a harmful pollutant. The chemical combines with rain to form acid rain, which is harmful to aquatic life in lakes and streams.

Cirrus thinning. Cirrus clouds are high, wispy ice clouds that absorb more heat than they reflect—so they act to increase the global temperature. Geoengineers think that pilotless drones could deliver desert dust or pollen into cirrus clouds. The dust would act as "seeds" for the formation of ice particles. As the ice particles spread out, the clouds break up. Then, less heat would be trapped, cooling Earth. However, this method could backfire. Too much cloud seeding could make the cirrus clouds persist and trap more heat!

Testing the salt spray technology

Marine brightening. Marine geoengineers think that fleets of ships pumping sea salt into the air could slow global warming. Ships could spray microscopic salt crystals high into the atmosphere where water vapor collects around them. This would thicken existing clouds with water droplets. The increased albedo from the clouds reflects more sunlight, and temperatures fall. But this proposed marine brightening risks changing Earth's weather patterns. Scientists using computer modeling found that brightening clouds over parts of the ocean reduced rainfall over the Amazon rain forest.

Termination shock occurs when you stop doing something useful only to find it was masking harmful effects. Reflecting heat to combat global warming seems useful, but it does nothing to stop the buildup of CO_2 emissions in Earth's atmosphere. Fossil fuels remain widespread even as CO_2 capture and storage technology develops. Greenhouse gases continue to increase in the atmosphere even if we can cool the planet using solar screens. If we stopped cloud seeding suddenly after 50 years without reducing or removing CO_2, termination shock will result. Earth's temperature would rise even more, making the problems with global warming much worse.

Chinese soldiers shoot cloud-seeding chemicals into the sky to make rain clouds over a drought-stricken area.

SPACE SUNSHADES

Space geoengineering involves using technology far from Earth to alter the climate. Geoengineers have plans to use spacecraft to change Earth's climate. Most of these radical plans focus on manipulating the amount of sunlight that reaches our planet.

Moondust could be used to provide a sun screen for Earth to cool global temperatures. Dust could be mined from the moon's surface by robots. Spacecraft can be used to spread moondust over Earth to create a giant orbiting dust cloud to block sunlight. This could work to slow global warming. But scientists have little idea of what would happen to the dust over time. Could it move out of orbit and become a problem elsewhere in space?

Mirror clouds. Geoengineers also have an idea to produce a sun-reflecting cloud from millions of thin mirrors launched into space over Earth. Spacecraft can launch thousands of tiny mirrors to disperse in an orbit where the gravitational pull of Earth and the sun are equal. This way, spacecraft will not be required to keep the cloud in position. Other geoengineers propose using a raft of bubbles to create this orbiting sun screen instead of mirrors. The bubbles could be made of special materials in space instead of being transported on rockets launched from Earth.

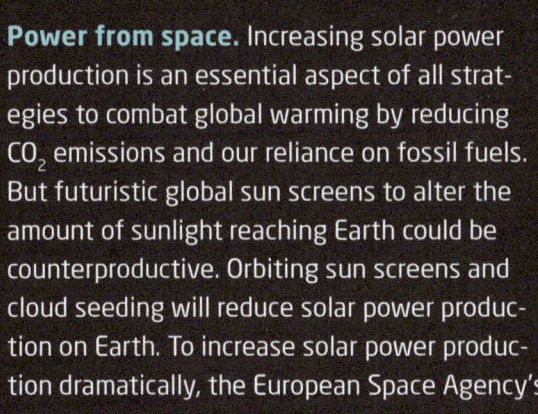

Power from space. Increasing solar power production is an essential aspect of all strategies to combat global warming by reducing CO_2 emissions and our reliance on fossil fuels. But futuristic global sun screens to alter the amount of sunlight reaching Earth could be counterproductive. Orbiting sun screens and cloud seeding will reduce solar power production on Earth. To increase solar power production dramatically, the European Space Agency's SOLARIS program plans to beam solar power to Earth from space. The SOLARIS program involves constructing an enormous orbiting solar farm using constellations of satellites. Each satellite will be equipped with arrays of PV cells to generate electricity. Satellites will transmit the electrical energy as microwaves to Earth. Special power plants on Earth will receive the transmissions and convert them back into usable electricity.

OCEAN SINK

Earth's oceans store incredible amounts of carbon. Oceans trap CO_2 from the atmosphere when it dissolves in surface waters, which then sinks into the deep ocean. Plankton in ocean waters also trap much of Earth's CO_2. When these tiny ocean organisms die, they sink to the ocean bottom, where the carbon they absorbed is trapped and stored. Geoengineers are finding new ways to enhance this ocean sink effect.

Fertilizing the oceans. The WhaleX project plans to fertilize the oceans by dumping tons of synthetic whale poop into the ocean around Australia! The synthetic poop—a blend of nitrogen, phosphorus, iron, and silica—will nourish the growth of carbon-absorbing phytoplankton. These tiny plant-like organisms use CO_2 dissolved in the seawater for photosynthesis. Dead phytoplankton sink to the seafloor where the carbon is trapped. Geoengineers have experimented fertilizing the oceans with iron, urea, and other substances that encourage phytoplankton growth. But they have yet to show that this process can remove enough CO_2 from the air to slow climate change. Other scientists point out that fertilizing the oceans can have unexpected consequences or disrupt delicate ocean ecosystems.

Coastal carbon capture. Earth's oceans are becoming more acidic from greenhouse gases. Excess CO_2 in the air generated from burning fossil fuels reacts with ocean water to make the water more acidic. This ocean acidification is harmful to many ocean creatures. The California-based company Vesta is producing a carbon-removing sand to combat ocean acidification and climate change. Vesta creates its artificial sand from the natural mineral olivine. Placed on a beach, the olivine sand reacts with CO_2 in the air to lock it up permanently. That sandy beach you visit on vacation may actually be reversing climate change!

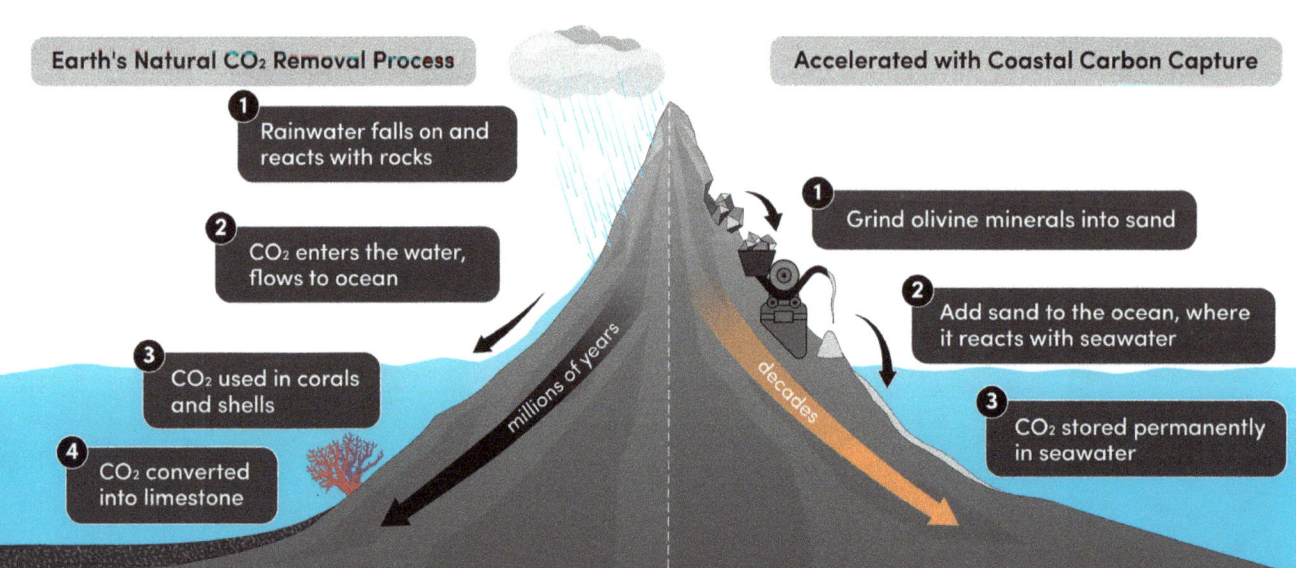

Moderating methane. Methane is a powerful greenhouse gas produced by decaying organic matter. The permanently frozen ground in Earth's Arctic regions holds vast amounts of trapped methane. As Earth warms, that ground is melting and releasing methane—accelerating global warming. In the Arctic Ocean today, plumes of methane bubble up from the seafloor. Geoengineers plan to moderate the effects of methane release by spraying a chemical named ferric chloride over the sea where the bubbles emerge. The chemical reacts with methane to form ferric hydroxide, which dissolves back into the seawater.

Seawilding is a process aimed to increase the area of coastal ecosystems that naturally absorb CO_2 from the air. Coastal ecosystems, including mangrove forests, salt marshes, and seagrass meadows, are known as blue carbon ecosystems. They absorb more CO_2 from the air compared to land ecosystems—so preserving and expanding these ecosystems helps moderate climate change. The British company HydroSurv uses uncrewed robot boats equipped with cutting-edge sensors to map, manage, and restore these vital blue carbon ecosystems.

5 ENERGY EFFICIENCY

ENERGY-EFFICIENT TECHNOLOGY

New carbon capture technology and carbon-neutral or carbon-free energy production are essential to reduce or even reverse global warming. But we have a long way to go. Most energy that we use today still comes from fossil fuels that emit CO_2 and other greenhouse gases. New technology can help reduce CO_2 emissions by using fossil fuels more efficiently until carbon-free energy tech can take over.

Increasing fossil fuel efficiency is not limited to switching off electronic devices or buying a car with better gas mileage. It involves changing the way we produce things, the materials we use to make things, and how we travel. Technology that uses energy and resources efficiently is known as green technology.

Green buildings use advanced new materials and technology to operate at peak energy efficiency. The Edge building in Amsterdam is one example. Opened in 2015, the Edge has been called the greenest building in the world. The office building has 30,000 sensors to detect occupancy, light level, temperature, and movement inside. Computer-controlled systems adjust the light and heat in different areas accordingly. Solar panels on one side generate carbon-free electricity that powers the building.

The Singapore-based company Gauzy produces advanced smart glass to efficiently maintain comfortable temperatures in buildings, lowering energy use. Smart glass can be switched from transparent to dark at the push of a button. In hot weather, the glass darkens to reduce solar heating. At the same time, the glass increases radiative cooling—a natural process where heat moves outside through surfaces to cool a room. The glass does the opposite to warm a room in cold weather.

GREEN TRANSPORTATION

Scientists and manufacturers are meeting the challenge of making transportation energy efficient in many ways. A bigger challenge is to radically redesign transportation to reach next-level efficiencies.

Flying-V. Air travel is a major source of CO_2 emissions today. New aircraft designs promise to make passenger airplanes more energy efficient—an important step toward a carbon-free future.

The Dutch TU Delft Flying-V is a radical new aircraft designed for energy-efficient long-distance air travel. The V-shaped aircraft reduces energy-using drag (air resistance) and is produced with high-tech materials to reduce its weight. The aircraft will carry 300 passengers on long trips using 20 percent less fuel than conventional airliners. The designers plan to convert the airliner to operate using carbon-free hydrogen fuel on future flights. It will be the world's first carbon-free airliner!

Hyperloop is a new energy-efficient technology for high-speed public transportation. Hyperloop vehicles are suspended by magnetic forces to float above a track within a vacuum tube. There is no friction between wheels and tracks as in a train and no air resistance (drag). This technology promises to move passengers or cargo with the speed of an airline using a fraction of the energy. In 2020, Virgin Hyperloop (now named Hyperloop One) completed its first passenger test in Las Vegas, Nevada. Passenger hyperloop systems are a long way off, however, since the current systems are designed mainly to transport cargo.

Solar autos. Electric automobiles with built-in solar panels are now entering production. The Lightyear 0 is a family car with solar panels covering its hood, roof, and tail. The panels generate enough power to drive up to 6,800 miles (10,943 kilometers) per year. You can drive farther by plugging it in to charge the batteries.

The Aptera solar electric vehicle (EV) can drive 40 miles (65 kilometers) powered by sunlight alone. The two-seated, three-wheeled EV has an aerodynamic dolphin-like shape—so it has less drag than boxier automobiles. Each of the wheels drives using its own energy-efficient motor. Aptera and other EVs are made of such light materials as carbon-fiber blends that are stronger than steel. Aptera weighs just 1,700 pounds (800 kilograms), so it uses less power to travel farther, carbon-free.

ENGAGE YOUR READER

Nonfiction writing often includes subject-specific vocabulary terms. Knowing the words related to the topic helps us understand the text itself.

When good readers come upon words they don't know well, they pause and try to figure them out. One tool they use is the glossary, like the one on page 4. Not every word can be defined in a glossary, though!

Authors know this, so they leave clues about words in the text. Next time you encounter a challenging word, stop and look for information about its meaning in the surrounding sentences. Sometimes authors define the term right there in the text! Other times, they'll compare the term to something you may already know. Authors even use punctuation like commas or dashes to clue you in to a word's meaning.

INSTRUCTIONS

1. Consider the list of challenge words and identify where each is used in the text. You can use the Index on page 48 to help you locate each term.

2. Explain how the author described each word. Ask yourself "what is happening in the text?" or "how is this word being used?" as you search for clues about their meanings.

3. Create your own definitions of the words. Don't just copy the dictionary definitions. Instead think about how you would tell a friend what each term means.

4. Add a visual representation for each word. Think about what you could draw that will help you remember what the words mean.

Visit www.worldbook.com/resources to download your own graphic organizer as well as other free resources!

CHALLENGE WORDS

- Potential energy
- Emissions
- Industrial
- Efficiency
- Hydrogen
- Biomass
- Battery
- Geoengineering

EXAMPLE

Challenge Word	Page(s)	Author's Description	Personal Definition	Visual Representation
Potential energy	7, 9, 13-16, 21-22	- the energy of motion stored - power when it is needed	Energy stored in an object that does not have motion, but could.	
Emissions				

INDEX

A
acidification, 40
aircraft, 14, 15, 18, 44
automobiles, 7, 10, 15, 23, 45

B
basalt, 13
batteries, 30-32, 45
biomass, 16, 19

C
carbon capture and storage (CCS), 12-13
carbon offset, 11
carbonate, 8, 10, 13, 16
cement, 16
climate change, 7, 10, 12, 13, 16, 17, 21, 25, 26, 35, 40, 41
clouds, 36-39
compressed (gas), 12, 28, 29, 35

D
direct air capture (DAC), 10, 11, 14, 17, 19

E
electrode, 9, 31
electrodialysis, 9
electrolysis, 22, 33
emissions (CO_2), 7, 9, 11, 13-16, 21, 22, 37, 39, 43, 44
enhanced oil recovery (EOR), 17

F
flues, 7-9
Formula 1, 15
fossil fuels, 7, 13-15, 17, 19, 21, 27, 29, 30, 37, 39, 40, 43
fusion, 20-21

G
generators, 24-25, 29
global warming, 7, 35-39, 41, 43
green technology, 15, 22, 43-44
greenhouse gases, 7, 10, 13, 14-16, 18, 26, 37, 40, 41, 43

H
hurricanes, 25, 35
hydrogen power, 21-23, 32, 33, 44
hydroxide, 8-10, 41

I
inject, 12, 17

M
methane, 18, 22, 41
mirrors, 15, 32, 38
modular, 9-11, 27, 31

N
nanomaterials, 18
nuclear power, 21, 26, 27, 32

O
oil, 12, 14, 17, 27
oxy-fuel, 7

P
photovoltaic (PV), 19, 24, 32, 39
phytoplankton, 40
post-combustion, 7
potential energy, 29, 32-33

R
reactor, 10, 11, 14, 15, 19, 21, 27, 32

S
salt, 28, 29, 32, 33, 37
seawater, 13, 21, 30, 40, 41
solar power, 15, 19, 21, 24, 26, 29, 30, 32, 39, 43, 45
solvents, 8, 16
sustainable, 30-31
syngas, 14, 15
synthetic fuels, 14-15

T
turbines, 24-25, 32-33

W
wind power, 21, 22, 24, 25, 29, 30, 32

Y
yeast, 15, 26

www.ingramcontent.com/pod-product-compliance
Lightning Source LLC
Chambersburg PA
CBHW041138170426
43198CB00023B/2982